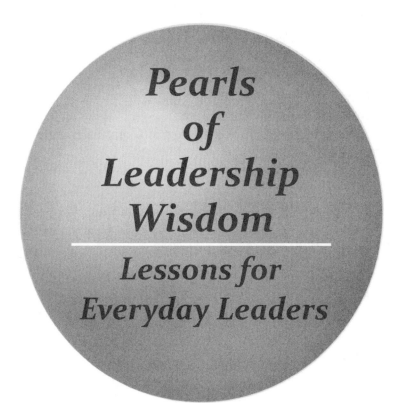

Pearls
of
Leadership
Wisdom

*Lessons for
Everyday Leaders*

by
Sandra Davis, Ph.D.

MDA LEADERSHIP CONSULTING
Advancing Great Leadership Since 1981

Pearls of Leadership Wisdom: Lessons for Everyday Leaders
©2012 MDA Leadership Consulting

Cover by Gieser Design
Interior Design by Patti Frazee
Interior Image of Pearl: ©istockphoto.com/malerapaso

ISBN: 978-0-9857503-0-5

MDA Leadership Consulting
150 S 5th St #3300
Minneapolis, MN 55402
www.mdaleadership.com

To order additional copies of this book,
visit www.MDALeadership.com

Acknowledgements

This book is dedicated to all the individuals who have shared the pains, struggles and triumphs of their leadership journeys. They have taught me so much and they are embedded in these pages. In tribute, I am thankful to all of my MDA colleagues and most especially my husband, Lynn, and our sons – Chris and Justin – who constantly teach me and keep me grounded.

—Sandra Davis

Table of Contents

About the Book's Cover Image

We chose this book's cover image because all leaders need to realize the ripple effects of every leadership choice. We hope each pearl in this book inspires you to reflect on your leadership style, consider your impact on others and ultimately reach the fullness of your leadership potential.

Prologue
and Reader's Guide

Welcome,

It's been said that leadership, like swimming, cannot be learned by reading a book.

Yet if there's a common element among *great* leaders, it is in how firmly they embrace *continuous* learning about leadership. Quite simply, great leaders are on a continuous quest to improve themselves — and their organizations. We all have the opportunity to learn every day!

That was my primary impetus for creating *Pearls of Leadership Wisdom* — to provide leaders at all stages of their development with a fresh perspective on ways they could potentially lead better. These pearls of leadership wisdom emerged from lessons learned in working with leaders like you over the past 30 years.

Why are there 30 pearls in this book? Because in 2011, MDA Leadership Consulting, the firm I co-founded, celebrated its 30th anniversary — an anniversary traditionally recognized with pearls. Thus, we provided the 30 pearls, one per week, as an anniversary gift to our clients and friends.

Pearls also correlate to some of life's most powerful leadership lessons. Consider how a pearl naturally forms. An irritant, perhaps an errant grain of sand, lodges inside an oyster. The irritant is bothersome, potentially painful, but definitely alien. The oyster reacts by forming a coating around the irritant until it creates a beautiful and treasured pearl.

Leadership lessons frequently start the same way — with an irritant — potentially painful, and often confusing, but which leads to treasured insight. We learn the most when we struggle with something, determine how to handle it, and find a better way the next time. Most likely, your own "pearls of leadership wisdom" have begun with an irritant: "Why isn't this working?" "Why don't people do what I wish they would do?" "How do I have an impact and stay true to my values?" Leadership lessons generally aren't comfortable, but ultimately, they're often quite valuable.

How to Use This Book

As I began writing these pearls, some "natural" categories began to emerge, based on either common dilemmas or possible points of pain. Irritants have a way of clustering together! Thus, the book's 30 pearls fall into one of the following six leadership categories:

Developing Self – *learning from your experiences*
Inspiring Leaders – *creating followership*
Executing Ideas – *making things happen*
Building Character – *being authentic*
Creating Culture – *developing great organizations*
Unlocking Talent – *building capabilities around you*

Rather than reading this book cover to cover in one sitting, you may find the greatest benefit by picking and choosing an intriguing title or leadership category, or by a current irritant in your leadership journey. Begin in the book's middle or even at the end. One pearl a day, or even one per week, might stimulate a new way for you to approach your role. Write in the book — there's plenty of white space to do that. Share a pearl with others. Create your own pearls. Use them to accelerate your own leadership education around the inevitable irritants that are part of the leadership journey!

My hope is that you find the pearls encouraging, empowering, and practical for everyday use. Many leaders have already shared the benefits they've discovered by applying these pearls in their everyday lives. Here are some examples of what these leaders have done with the 30 pearls:

- Brought a new pearl to biweekly staff meetings for group discussion
- Sent one to an individual who was struggling with an issue covered in that pearl
- Forwarded a pearl to her management, because of similar issues her organization faced
- Created a newsletter column related to a pearl
- Started a journal of leadership reflections, based on the pearls, to capture lessons learned
- Used the pearls as part of mentoring and coaching conversations

You will find your own ways to use these pearls, and I hope you make them your own. I wish you great joy and success in your own leadership journey!

Best regards,

Sandra Davis, Ph.D.
CEO, MDA Leadership Consulting

The Leader You Will Be Tomorrow Is Not the Leader You Are Today

G reat leaders are on a "leadership journey." They learn, grow, evolve, develop, and find new ways to lead in an ever-evolving leadership environment. While the oft-heard expression, "you can't teach an old dog new tricks," may subtly tempt us to opt out of active learning, we have an enormous capacity to change and develop. Becoming a better leader tomorrow means proactively striving to do so today.

Ideas for Action

While it may seem tough to find time to be intentional about learning, we know practice makes perfect for leadership effectiveness, just as it does for anything worth doing well. Every day we have the chance to learn, if we just take it. Look at the events, interactions, conversations, and meetings you will encounter in the next week. How can you tackle them in a new way, rather than just relying on what may have worked (or not) in the past?

Consider creating a meaningful and compelling leadership development plan, focused on one or two areas for growth. Base one of the areas on a strength and find new ways to use it; make the second area something outside of your "comfort zone" that will help you stretch and grow. Write down and share your goals to increase your likelihood for success. One leader I know consistently writes down what she has learned and how she will apply it in the future.

You can advance your leadership journey by making your learning intentional and opportunistic. Here's to the leader you will be tomorrow!

Notes

1. for all the Coaching I have never really created an LDP
   - Create an LDP
   - read _all_ Susan's notes
2. Do _not_ beat up yourself!
3. Start by doing; Step 1 is to go easy on your peers; Step 2 is to fix problems.

Notes

2

Your Impact on Followers Trumps Having the "Right Stuff"

By definition traits are. We headed in right direction

Decades ago, leadership pundits debated over what constitutes the "right stuff" for leaders. They saw leadership as residing in individual traits and characteristics; they paid attention to what the individual leader brought to the party. Leadership then and to some extent now was about having the right confidence, presence, intelligence, social skills, or strategic ability. Finding someone with the "right stuff" guaranteed one had found an effective leader.

Personal characteristics form a foundation, but leadership is really about what happens in the interaction between the leader and his or her followers. Turn the camera around; instead of watching the performance of a leader in front of a group, record the reactions and engagement of the audience. That means no matter how much

Do we ask the right ? & of EEO re: Managers? Should we survey?

you try to perfect your own performance, the real proof of your effectiveness lies in how others react and respond to you.

Ideas for Action

While not a practical idea for everyday action, we know one leader who had two video cameras operating during a presentation he made. One camera recorded him while the other focused on his audience. He measured his impact by how engaged and responsive his audience was, not by his own presence or absence of "uhs" and "ums."

While creating a video of your interactions is likely impractical, there are many ways for you to find out the effectiveness of your interpersonal interactions. Instead of taking this video example literally, consider what you can do on an ongoing basis to learn how engaged others are with you.

Ask for candid, objective feedback about your impact. Especially ask about your interpersonal effectiveness: empathy, approachability, respect, listening, and communication. Ask one of your trusted team members to pay attention to how others respond to you at a meeting. What were your strengths? Where could you grow? This is an ongoing trait of great leaders: they continue to solicit input from others to make "course corrections" in their leadership journeys.

The impact you have on others cannot be changed overnight, but you can build a habit of constantly learning how you affect others. Use the "right stuff" you have and make sure it reso-nates with others in ways that get them engaged with following you.

Notes

Create a Checklist:

- ☑ Empathy
- ☑ Approachability
- ☑ Respect
- ☐ Listening
- ☐ Communication

Great Leaders "Mind the Gap"

If you have traveled on subways in the U.K., where this phrase originated, you will have heard someone say, "mind the gap," in a lovely, lilting British accent. It calls us to pay attention to the physical gap between the edge of the platform and the train car.

There is a similar gap between intention and action, which great leaders understand is their job to bridge. Passion, great ideas, and hope only carry us so far; true achievement rides on putting these imperatives into practical action.

Ideas for Action

Passion and hope are wonderful attributes for a leader. They inspire others and compel them to follow. But passion alone is not enough. Like Icarus, the mythological Greek character whose desire to reach the sun on his wax wings proved his undoing, those whose passions and intentions are not translated into real plans that others can follow run the risk of burning out themselves — or their team members.

Recognize first that your passions, intentions, and hopes are not plans. Effective, results-oriented leaders understand the gap between knowing what to do and actually doing it. They engage their teams in conversations about "how will we make that happen?" and follow their enthusiasm for a great business idea with demands for plans that detail the specifics of execution. They track progress on goals, encourage their teams to develop contingency plans, and help them adapt and adjust as they encounter inevitable obstacles and unknowns.

Ask yourself: "What do we need to do to mind the gap? Where do we need a bridge between what we believe we need to do and our plans for execution? Where do we have passions and dreams in place with no plans behind them?" By engaging your team in truly minding the gap, you will spark others to achieve great things in reality and keep your collective passions from flaming out.

For further reading on this topic, I suggest the book, *Execution: The Discipline of Getting Things Done*, by Larry Bossidy and Ram Charan.

Notes

Notes

Leaders Live By: "Officers Eat Last"

If you served in the military, or know someone who has, you may be familiar with the phrase, "Officers eat last." Popular in the Marine Corps, the phrase expresses the practice that a leader first makes sure the troops are fed before he or she joins the table.

In 1981, when Pete Meyer and I started MDA, he advocated this as an MDA value. Having served in the Army, he told me the military taught him his primary job was to look out for his people.

Now, when I hear board members say they want a leader who puts the needs of the organization ahead of personal gain, I am reminded of Pete's commitment. Simply put, a leader's first job is to look out for the good of the organization. The most highly respected leaders consistently put the needs of their organization ahead of their own.

Ideas for Action

I am reminded of the story of Aaron Feuerstein, the former CEO of Massachusetts-based Malden Mills Industries, maker of Polartec polar fleece fabric. After his Malden Mills factory burned down in late 1995, Feuerstein achieved widespread acclaim by continuing to pay his employees' salaries while the factory was being rebuilt.

While not all officers "eat last," the good ones like Feuerstein, do. It's a matter of understanding that part of your role as a leader is to do what's best for the entire organization. What are you doing to support the people who work for you? How are you finding out what's important to them? People have an intrinsic need for meaning and relevance in their work; what are you doing to help them see the connections between what they do and the goals of the larger organization?

While you need to consider how you show your employees that you care, sustaining and strengthening your organization also requires you to make the tough calls. For example, if you can't change the behavior of someone who is an "energy drainer" on your team, you need to step up to take action, so that your team has a chance to become high-performing.

Being focused on others first clearly extends to high-pressure times. When you and your team face difficult or time-consuming assignments, ask yourself: "What can I do to help? What might I tackle myself to be a visible part of the workload? Am I treating those who work for me the way I would like to be treated? Am I ensuring they have the resources to get the job done?"

As you consider your role and responsibilities as a leader, never forget the value of being focused on your team. Others will notice who or what you put first!

Notes

Discern the Times for Courage and Conviction: "It's My Call."

Anyone in the midst of leading change knows intimately how critical it is to involve and engage others in decision making and planning. Decisions and choices are complex; more voices are typically better than one.

Yet part of the art of leadership is discerning when consensus and collaboration aren't the right choice. Crises, financial choices, and dicey personnel matters often require courageous action. These are moments in time for you to be decisive, to make what you believe is the right choice and even more importantly, to own it and say, "It's my call."

One of our clients told us about walking away from an acquisition that several people on her team wanted to pursue. Later, when a competitor snapped up the target company, she heard internal rumors that the "senior team missed a chance." In a subsequent meeting with the company's managers, she addressed the topic head-on, saying, "Right or wrong, I personally made that call." Are you leading with that degree of courage and ownership?

Ideas for Action

Be clear about your typical and "fallback" decision-making styles. Some leaders thrive on consensus decision making, some convene a group of "out of the box" thinkers, some turn to experts, some trust their own judgment or experience most, some turn to detailed analytics, and some rely on the chain of command to bring an answer forward. No matter what your typical approach happens to be for decision making, the critical skill is to discern the moments in time when it's your call.

At a trade association meeting, I heard a former chief marketing officer describe how he helped change his company's business from a film manufacturer to a company that manages and moves images and information. This fundamental shift required the company's employees to think differently and become more innovative. In one of his first meetings with his marketing team, he urged them to make choices, move quickly, and experiment. He said, "Ask yourself:

'If I try this, is anyone going to die?' If the answer is 'no,' then try it."

The critical skill is discerning when it's your call. One critical "blinder" that can keep you from discerning that moment is worry: worry about being liked, worry about being able to keep others' approval, or worry about making a wrong choice. So ask yourself: "Do I have any internal blinders that keep me from discerning when it's time to step up and make a call? Do I have any blinders that cause me to postpone or delay a decision that's really mine to make? Am I looking for confirmation just to feel better? Is anyone going to die if I make this call?"

At day's end, your team — and others in your organization — will respect you more for having the courage to make a choice.

Notes

Encourage the Truth-Tellers

I t's the irony of leadership: the higher you go on the leadership ladder, the more difficult it can be to know or discern the whole truth about what is happening in the organization.

I recall vividly a conversation with a COO who said, "A month ago it was announced I would be the next CEO, and the next day, people were already treating me differently." He went on to say how aware he was that others were "managing" him. People were being careful about what they told him. It is not that he suspected colleagues of lying to him, it was his awareness that they would decide how much to tell him and when. He was concerned about the "shad-ings" of truth that occur in the workplace each day. Would people agree with him because of his role? Would they tell him his ideas were off base? Might they dismiss or withhold vital information to get along or get ahead?

Whether your organization is small or large and whether you are the CEO or the head of a function, the same dynamic exists — people will at times relate to you based on your role. By being aware of it, you can develop mechanisms for encouraging and discerning the truth. Even more starkly, ask yourself: "Who do I have who will tell me the truth?"

Ideas for Action

Understand that organizational truth-telling is both a cultural and individual dynamic. We make individual decisions about the information we opt to share (or not); however, our roots and workplace environment can also affect our truth-telling orientation. Were you raised to try not to hurt someone's feelings? Are you reluctant to be completely candid, out of concern for others' sentiments? Do you give too much power away to those in authority? Do you work in an environment where discrepant opinions are squashed? Do you ever opt out of speaking up out of concern for your job security and career?

Truth-telling is a two-way street. Start by examining your own transparency. Are you as candid with colleagues as you can or could be, in order to provide them with the best opportunities for success? On the receiving end, are you open to all kinds of information, to ensure it is readily shared with you? Do you make it easy for others to bring anything and everything to you?

Work hard to identify and break down barriers to truth-telling within your organization. Recognize that your role itself (not just how you behave) can cause others to be reluctant to give you information. It's partly your job to help them be comfortable with you.

Get out of your cubicle or closed-door office, engage in genuine conversations with individuals at all levels of the organization and show that you are interested in what they think. Truly listen and don't shut down information that you would rather not hear.

When someone brings you something you don't want to hear, be open and non-judgmental. Encourage candor: "I need to hear your honest opinion on this, and I will do the same"; "What else are people saying in the organization that I need to hear or know?"

By finding ways for your colleagues to speak the truth, you provide one of the greatest gifts of all in the workplace: an environment where people express their honest sentiments — and are championed for doing so.

Notes

Collaboration Wins

Even as little as five years ago, many corporate boards MDA worked with did not have "collaboration" on their list of preferred senior executive skills or traits. In fact, the more competitive an individual, the more positively that individual was viewed. That has changed. Collaborative skills have significantly moved up the ladder.

In the last year, every board I worked with on CEO succession told me they needed someone who could collaborate internally and build business alliances externally. In a recent survey of 950 global business professionals, collaboration was identified as the most important factor in overall business performance — more than twice the impact as the next-nearest factor (a company's market aggressiveness). In addition, a survey from McKinsey shows that companies using collaborative Web technologies to connect the internal efforts of their employees and to extend the organization's reach to customers, partners, or suppliers, gain greater market share and higher margins. That says it all.

The world is too complex for pure competitiveness to be the key to success. Success and collaboration are synonymous; it is about connecting with others so you can create effective and rich solutions.

Ideas for Action

If collaboration is the ticket to winning, then you need to figure out your key collaborators. One of the criticisms we often hear about an organization's culture is that there are silos everywhere. Furthermore, employees quickly see pockets of competition.

You have the power to change that. Think about which individuals and which groups are collectively integral to the work you do. Instead of plotting how to win in your sphere of influence or function, consider who else has a vested interest in your decisions. That includes peers, customers, suppliers, and other business units.

Reach out to these individuals, find out what they think, test ideas with them and seek their input on what you are doing. Yes, you may be "competing" for resources, but the goal is to win for the broader organization, not just for yourself or your team. Reach out to customers or alliance partners. Use customer input and feedback to shape current offerings and future products. Treat them as partners in your business endeavors, not just "buyers."

Look inside and critique yourself. Are you acting like a solo athlete competing in a sprint or like a member of a mountaineering team in which interdependence is the only way to survive and summit? When is the last time you showed your desire to collaborate by intentionally reaching out to others who share the same goals, but may have different styles, varying perspectives, or other skills? If you demonstrate a mentality of "I am going to win no matter what," you may find others avoiding you.

When you or your team members experience conflicts or setbacks, proactively address and resolve these issues in ways to enhance all-around success. Coach your key team members on how to build relationships across groups. While you can coach others on ways to achieve greater collaboration, demonstrating collaboration rather than a win-at-all-costs competitive spirit will have a great positive impact on those around you.

Being competitive is a good thing — especially as you determine how to win in the market and for your company. Being collaborative is even more important; ultimately, others will seek you out because you show a genuine interest in their success. Stand tall for modeling a spirit of cooperation.

Notes

Go Viral:
Promote Optimism and Hope

We live in an unpredictable world. Not only have the economic challenges of the last few years driven that fact home, but natural disasters — earthquakes, tornados, and floods — make it all the more apparent. "Improbable" events are actually common.

While no one can predict or control the future, we want leaders who can give us a spirit of optimism and hope about it.

When I ask individuals what they want in their next leader, I hear statements about someone who can thrive amid uncertainty, move forward despite setbacks and keep a positive outlook no matter the challenges. No one wants to work with someone who preaches doom and gloom. More importantly, part of a leader's role is to convey hope and optimism about the future and the collective ability of a team to deal with challenges.

Your beliefs about possibilities are contagious, like a social media-driven viral marketing campaign. I like Colin Powell's statement, "Perpetual optimism is a force multiplier."

Ideas for Action

First, explore your own attitudes and feelings about things that happen to you. When negative things happen, do you find ways to learn from them and move on, or do you try to find something or someone to blame? People who find ways to learn and then apply the lessons for the future have an abundance of "learned optimism." When you envision an end result for you and your team, can you imagine multiple ways to achieve it? People who imagine themselves coping positively with all kinds of outcomes can give others a sense of calm and hope about the future as well.

Next, seek ways to visibly show your inward hope and optimism outwardly to others. This is not about only showcasing the positive. Deliver clear, informed, and well-grounded messages that paint a picture of how you foresee things. Candidly bring up challenges you anticipate and get your team thinking about how they will deal with them. Proactively solicit input from others on your vision and/or challenges — the better to engage them in your line of thinking. Your team members need to believe they can and will cope well with whatever obstacles the future brings them.

When a setback occurs, promote an attitude of learning. What happened? How does it affect our goal? How can we work around this? What else can we do to get back on track? Don't let your team become a victim of circumstance; help them be champions of action! When you see individuals on your team who show particular resilience or optimism, highlight their efforts so that others can see what a difference they make.

Start telling the stories that show why you are optimistic and hopeful about the future. Stories make your aspirations come alive. Even entire companies trade in hope. For example, in its annual employee meetings and annual reports, Medtronic regularly shares its successes in medical technology through individual patient stories.

Ultimately, by embracing your role in promoting hope and optimism, you will give others confidence in their ability to cope with uncertainty. It's contagious!

To further explore your own attitudes about hope and optimism, I suggest reading *Learned Optimism: How to Change Your Mind and Your Life*, by Dr. Martin E.P. Seligman.

Notes

9

Know Your Talent Right(s)

Collectively, we spend precious little time on talent reviews, human capital audits, and dialogue about people. Yet in an increasingly knowledge-based economy, we all know talent matters; it has a distinct, discernable value to an organization.

An analysis of S&P 500 companies revealed that only $1 of every $6 of "market-to-book" value is from financial or physical assets. The remainder is from intangible assets — principally, an organization's talent. That translates right into your role as a leader and what you do to grow and preserve your organization's talent assets. The shorthand for your role says you need to have the "right people on the bus."

I think it is helpful to realize there is more than one "right" when it comes to decisions about people. Recently, when I was on a panel with the head of talent for a Fortune 50 company, he noted that his company considers talent decisions in terms of five rights. That suddenly made the concept richer for me. Think about the right person with the right skills in the right job with the right timing for the right reason. We can change the dialogue about "the right people on the bus" by considering all five rights.

Ideas for Action

Spend time to do a real talent audit for your team or function. As a starter, ask yourself about each individual player. Do I have the right person:

- with the right values and cultural fit?
- with the right kinds of skills and skill levels?
- in the right job—match between the individual and the job?
- with the right timing—today or tomorrow?
- for the right reasons and the needs you are meeting — yours, the individual's, or the organization's?

Use this audit to determine whether you really have the right people and resources to meet your function's goals. If not, you have changes to make.

Face the facts. If you discover that you have too many grade-"C" players who lack a combination of several of these "rights," you need to find a solution. Some of these people are simply in the wrong job, some may not be a good cultural fit, some may not have or be able to learn the skills you need for the future, and some may be tolerated because they are well-liked. But every high-performing team needs more "A" players — those individuals you wish you could clone! Do you have any and what are you doing to keep them engaged? Are you helping the "B" players learn, grow, and achieve their full potential?

Sometimes a visual says it all. I recall a client who used the common red-yellow-green talent chart to look at performance and potential. Red indicated low; yellow was solid; and green meant both high performance and high potential. The learning came when all business units were displayed side-by-side. The business unit with the strongest results had lots of greens and no reds, while the business unit that was struggling had a chart filled primarily with yellows dotted here and there with a few reds. That color-charting talent audit led this company to action.

Use the five rights to talk about all people decisions: *promotions*, *lateral moves*, *hiring*, *constituting new teams*, *downsizing*, and *developmental moves*. Block time on your calendar to focus on talent and talk with your peers about their teams and how they see some of your players. Keep the talent dialogue front and center, even as you deal with competitive challenges and customer issues.

Remember that first statistic — almost 80% of business value can be tied to human assets. You can impact that value.

In the coming years, talent quality will increasingly separate the high-performing organizations from the lesser-performing organizations. Be sure you have the right talent in place and ensure it is consistently put to the test.

Notes

Notes

Culture Trumps Strategy

Has this ever happened to you? You are in the midst of leading a change initiative and you suddenly discover that despite what people said they would do, it isn't happening.

Finding the root cause for puzzling employee behavior is not simple; root causes can be elusive. One possible culprit is the organization's culture. As Peter Drucker, the late writer and prognosticator about modern management once said: "Culture eats strategy for breakfast." Think about how often a strategic initiative succeeds or fails based on its fit with an organization's culture.

One of my colleagues, Bob Barnett, reminded me of work we did helping a large media company define and reinforce its values. Those values caused their CEO to say "no" to an acquisition during the due diligence process, precisely because the values and culture of the two organizations were polar opposites. Later, his successor decided to move forward with the same acquisition; five years later, they are still struggling to integrate and realize the value of their purchase. Culture wins.

Ideas for Action

Culture — a collection of values and norms shared by people or groups in an organization — governs how we interact with each other. Become tuned to the character and culture of the organization (or team) you are leading.

Culture is easiest to see when you first join a new organization or work group. Try finishing this sentence: "It's interesting; people here always seem to...." If you have been in the organization or team for a while, think of the rules that seem to exist about how decisions are made, how communication is handled, what behavior is rewarded and who is seen as the most valued. Ask trusted colleagues, compare notes, and write it down. What do the most respected leaders value, and what do they do? Culture ultimately comes through in actions, not words.

Here's another fun way to think of your organization's culture: try playing the game "organizational blasphemy." Get two or three colleagues together to think of a statement that would be blasphemous in your world. For example, here at MDA, a blasphemy would be "go ahead and schedule over that; it's just a client meeting!" The truthful opposite of the blasphemy reflects your organization's culture.

Now think about that change effort you are leading. How will your culture either work to support or kill your initiative? If you realize that there are cultural elements that will work against what you are planning, you need to engage others in figuring out what you can do to start to reinforce new behaviors. If there are no systems to reinforce or reward new behaviors, the old ones will be the fallback.

In your day-to-day work, don't believe the myth that the best ideas always win in the end. Instead, winning ideas and strategies are typically generated by those who best understand and function within the cultural milieu of their organizations. Just as I have never seen a leader who's a cultural mismatch take on his or her company's culture and ultimately win, I have often seen executives succeed wildly due to their keen cultural awareness.

Remember that culture can't be changed by itself. You are better off working to change systems, processes, and people; in other words, bringing about cultural change through other means. Engage your own team in thinking about culture and the role it plays in the initiatives you are leading. By doing so, you harness the good and help people learn the new behaviors or norms that may need to be part of the future.

Notes

Stretch Beyond
the Predictable

In the early years of MDA, one of my clients was a senior executive whose leadership style intrigued me. People went above and beyond for her; it was as if she had a "secret sauce." She was passionate, energetic, unrelenting, and unafraid of touting audacious goals. But there was something more: rather than leading based on transactions, she was transformative instead.

Transactional leaders carefully define goals and anticipated rewards. They ask, "What are you looking for in your work and how can I help you succeed?" While that is a reasonable conversation for a leader, it offers a predictable exchange of this for that — a transaction.

Transformational leaders go one step further. Had my client asked only, "What do you believe you can do?" her team's goals would have been reasonable and comfortable. Instead, she painted a compelling picture of the future that inspired her team to want to achieve it. She saw what was possible, person by person, and challenged each to achieve in ways they might not have chosen on their own. She literally "transformed" them individually.

Ideas for Action

What are you doing to paint a compelling picture of the future that inspires individuals to go beyond what they otherwise might choose? Transformational leaders somehow make the impossible seem realistic.

Once you and your team have a shared vision, link that vision with specific actions for each team member. Make your delegation to individual team members less directive ("Your job is to complete this part for us.") and more vision-oriented ("I can imagine you really doing well by taking the lead on this piece."). Don't be afraid to challenge someone to step up into a new role — if you believe they can do it.

Consistently express confidence in the individual abilities of your team members to achieve or go above and beyond. It's like the Pygmalion effect in management: people have a habit of living up to (or down to) your expectations. The more you convey either directly or subtly that an individual is not good enough, they aren't. The more you show your confidence in their ability to rise to the occasion, the more they do.

A senior leader told me that an inflection point in her career was when her manager said, "Let's look for a management role for you because I think you would be great at it." At the time she would have never raised her hand to ask for that kind of assignment, because she had not yet thought about it as possible. He helped her literally transform her career.

Know that there is a downside to unrelenting transformation. I have seen powerful transformational leaders burn their people out. Constantly stretching to go above and beyond is thrilling and exhausting. As you and your team achieve successes, take time to recognize and celebrate them. Give yourself and others time to recover and celebrate before you conquer the next new "impossible" feat.

By proactively and incrementally working to imagine the best for your team members, you will achieve the true hallmark of a transformational leader: cultivating followers who are consistently willing to stretch beyond the predictable to achieve the seemingly impossible.

Notes

The Art of Coaching

Recently, our two-year-old granddaughter stood grinning at the plate, bat in hand, hoping to hit the same kind of backyard Wiffle Ball screamer she just saw her eight-year-old brother launch. He was helping her grip the bat, stand at the plate, and time her "swing." All the while he was saying, "Audrey, you can do it." There, in our backyard, was the real truth about coaching.

I'm not talking about *coach* (the noun), which many use as a synonym for leader. I'm talking about the art of coaching, which is part of a great leader's repertoire. As my colleague and master coach, Joe Volker, likes to say, "Coaching is the art of keeping someone on their growing edge."

To coach means to teach, to guide, to educate, or to set up the right conditions for learning. Coaching is all about behavior change. It requires four elements: a good relationship, a desired goal (challenge), a willing learner, and a great environment to practice in (support).

There were all four, right in front of my eyes.

Audrey laughed with excitement when she barely ticked the ball forward — she dropped the bat and clapped her hands. Running after you hit? That must be next week's lesson.

Ideas for Action

How are you coaching others at work? Take stock of the four critical elements and how you are using them:

- building the relationship (I would call it an alliance between you and the learner)
- goal-setting (creating the challenge)
- ensuring you have a willing learner
- providing the support for the inevitable successes and failures of learning something new.

All challenge with no support leads people to be afraid to try; all support with no challenge means the goal is too easy. Think about how you challenge and how you support: what's the ledger look like for you?

Let's assume you have a willing learner who is asking for feedback. Providing feedback is one of the skills at the heart of effective coaching. The process itself is challenging and rewarding. Done well, feedback is a powerful force for learning. Handled poorly (or more commonly, not at all), it leads the learner to either guessing or resisting. A Major League Baseball coach was once fired because of his alleged inability to provide useful feedback to his players.

One rule of thumb to follow is that feedback is a thoughtful gift: Assume people want to know about their impact. One of the most common complaints at all levels of an organization is: "I don't get enough feedback from my manager." A second rule of thumb is to stay away from labels; focus on the behavior and its impact, and be as non-judgmental as you can. Third, tie your feedback to things that make a difference in terms of your team's goals, and link these goals to organizational performance.

One way to know if you are being specific enough with both positive and constructive feedback is to use the DESC method: Describe the behavior; reveal your Emotional reaction to it; be Specific about what you want to happen in the future and describe the (positive) Consequences of continuing or changing the behavior. Here's an example:

Describe: "I have noticed you arriving late for most of our team meetings."

Emotion: "I am frustrated, because it wastes everyone's time."

Specific: "We all need you to be here at the start of our meetings."

Consequences: "When you do that, your colleagues will know you want to be part of this team, and they will respect what you have to say."

You'll find the DESC model works for positive feedback too. "Way to keep watching the ball, Audrey. Next time, you can run over there to first base." Priceless!

Here's to great coaching being in your repertoire, too!

Notes

Notes

Own Your Own Mistakes

I sn't it refreshing when someone says, "I'm sorry, that was my fault"? No excuses, no rationale, no long-winded explanations — just a simple apology. If you want to gain others' support and be authentic, then be willing to admit to a mistake you know you made and hear how your actions may have disappointed someone.

All of us are fallible in different ways — it's in our human nature. What separates truly great leaders from the rest of the crowd is their ability to humbly and sincerely apologize. It's not complicated, yet somehow we make it difficult.

Consider the public acclaim that Warren Buffet received when he acknowledged some investing mistakes ("I did some dumb things."). Taking responsibility for your actions enhances trust within your work and your family relationships.

Building Character

Ideas for Action

In my view, there are four kinds of mistakes: honest mistakes, errors of omission, errors of human nature, and trial-and-error mistakes.

An honest mistake is a misstep — something you did not intend to do, but did. Examples range from accidentally double-booking your time, forgetting a meeting, failing to let someone know about a decision you made, making a poor hiring decision, or sending a confidential e-mail to the wrong person. It's an example of courage when an individual has the self-confidence and humility to admit they made an error.

Honest mistakes are a part of life, in ways small and large. A client told me about how her boss responded to a mistake she was devastated about. She had made a simple math error that could ultimately cost her company $20 million. When her response was to submit a letter of resignation, her boss rejected it, saying, "I just spent $20 million training you, and now you want to leave?"

A second type of mistake is an error of omission. It may not be visible to others, but it is to you. These mistakes fit under the heading of "could've, should've, would've." Maybe it was something you neglected to say or do that you learned from in retrospect. These are preventable when you choose to act rather than wait.

A third type of mistake is caused by human

nature. We all have personality traits that can trip us up. For example, you may be a perfectionist, overly independent, too confident, an under-communicator, mistrustful of others, etc. — fill in the list with your own foible. If you know what can derail you or cause leadership problems for you personally, you can take steps to prevent damaging situations or relationships.

Finally, I wish we made more mistakes of the fourth variety: trial and error. Trial-and-error mistakes are simply part of learning; you may make them when you try something new or stretch beyond your comfort zone into uncharted territory. You may not know how something is going to turn out, but go ahead and try. Then learn from what happens. If we all expect perfection the first time into uncharted waters, we'll never go there.

Whether you're addressing a mistake of your own or working with a colleague who's erred, determine how you can turn the event into a teachable moment. It's a matter of trust and authenticity.

Notes

Use Your Intuition

"**P**resent the business case!" I hear that constantly when working with leaders. If you want to sell someone on your terrific idea, outline the facts and rationale behind it: a compelling business story is persuasive, yet decisions can't be reduced to facts and data alone. Intuition is a powerful resource — especially if you bring it to the surface and learn to trust it.

Brian, an executive, told me how he learned too late of the value of intuition. His company was in the midst of due diligence for a potential acquisition. On paper, the target company deal looked good and its leadership was saying the right things. Brian thought something about the deal didn't "feel right," but the facts were so convincing that he let it go. After the deal was inked, his company discovered the owner had fudged the books. The acquisition was a mistake, and Brian realized he had ignored his intuition. The power of his intuitive insights never entered the picture.

Ideas for Action

Think of times when your intuition has proven eerily accurate: perhaps you had a "sense" about a particular person or work situation, and later discovered you were right. Whether you're making a business decision, building a work team, or trying out a new idea, open yourself to the power of your intuition.

In a basic way, there are two primary ways we reach conclusions. One is based on reasoned analysis, in which we systematically gather facts and narrow them down to reach a conclusion. The other is based on intuitive analysis — a mental process that allows you to see or even imagine patterns in information. Intuition literally helps you connect the dots among seemingly disparate data points. Science is increasingly discovering how our brains analyze and connect information based on both types of analysis.

Logic or intuition? It is not an either/or world. Simply think in terms of using all of your brain power to reach a conclusion. Know that intuition often becomes more accurate over time because it unconsciously taps prior knowledge and experience. Similarly, intuition may be less reliable when you are operating in a brand-new arena.

Recently, while sitting in a cab in New York City during rush hour, I was amazed how the veteran cab driver managed to glide through and around traffic. How could he do that? His mastery of New York streets was based on both reasoned analysis (knowing which alternative routes would lead him to my destination) as well as intuition (an opening that told him the right lane was going to be faster than the middle lane). My intuition would have been worthless at that point — I did not have the mental map to make helpful connections. But I have other mental maps and experiences that do allow me to make connections.

Using your intuition does not mean you always have to follow it. In Brian's example, the problem was that he never voiced his intuitive doubts. Intuition needs a voice and benefits from you making it accessible; first to yourself and then to others. Familiarize yourself with your own intuitive capacity by saying or writing down your intuition to give it credence: "I have a hunch this product team is going down the wrong path," or "Even though everyone is not in agreement, something tells me this is a better choice."

Keep track of the quality of your intuitive thinking to better gauge where and when it's best applied. I have a sense you'll be pleased with the results!

Notes

Seek Diverse Points of View

We naturally like people who are like ourselves. After all, it's self-validating to hear from those who sound much like you. Yet the best leaders are those who proactively seek input from a variety of people — especially those with differing backgrounds, knowledge, and perspectives — to assess risks and make better-informed decisions.

President Abraham Lincoln famously created a Cabinet not of his friends, but rather of major political figures, some of whom (such as Salmon P. Chase) were his chief rivals. Although Lincoln valued friendships, he did not place them above the need for effective public service.

Leaders who surround themselves with those who offer contrary points of view not only tend to make better decisions, they also help create a workplace of individuals unafraid to raise contrarian views. By contrast, leaders who create "echo chambers" of like-minded associates often overestimate their expertise and underestimate the consequences of suboptimal decision making.

Ideas for Action

A diverse workplace should be a way of being, not a way of counting. When hiring or assembling work teams, strive to include a variety of people who feel emboldened to offer their own perspectives.

Be on guard against surrounding yourself solely with those you like or those who share your way of thinking. When interviewing candidates for clients I will sometimes jot a note to myself in the margin: "Be careful! She's like you." I do this to ensure I'm assessing the candidate against the right set of criteria, and not simply based on likability.

When meeting those unlike you, strive to not make assumptions that may not be well-founded. How often do we dismiss people based on a preconceived label? "Oh, he's an X" or "She's a Y." Instead, seek to understand such individuals — who they are and what they might bring to your dialogue or efforts.

I love becoming better acquainted with foreign languages because I believe they reflect a thought culture. German, for example, is very structured, while Chinese words only have meaning in context. English, on the other hand, is based on a diversity of other languages and ideas, which explains in part why it's been adopted as the global language of business.

Just as English reflects a diversity of perspectives and is more widely accepted as a result, so, too, can your workforce reflect a diversity of viewpoints, and thus become more effective. To paraphrase a saying, diversity is the spice of life!

Notes

Laughter, Fun, and Work

It was the middle of January and three of us from MDA were having dinner at a quiet restaurant in Minot, North Dakota. Suddenly there was a commotion on the other side of the room; we glanced across and saw George Burns, the celebrity comedian and writer, who was in his late 90s at the time. Later I had a chance to ask Mr. Burns to what he attributed his longevity. Without hesitating, he said, "I have always chosen to do what I love; work should be fun, not a chore!" That encounter was years ago, but his observation still rings true.

Of course, there are aspects of any job that may not be exciting; but overall, if work is not fun, find something else. Just think of these implications: you spend at least half of your waking hours at work each day, and if those aren't fun, they certainly won't be enjoyable for the individuals who work with you. Laughter belongs at work. There's a time to be serious for sure, but organizations that take time for fun, play, and laughter become great places to work.

Ideas for Action

Remember that you as a leader set the tone for the balance between seriousness and fun. Let others see the value you place on both. Find the humor even in small things that happen; remember that laughing at yourself makes you more human, too.

If most of your team is in one location, wander the halls and listen. Is there ever any laughter? A new CEO and I once walked through groups of fully occupied, but deathly quiet cubicles at his company. "Do you hear that?" he asked. I confessed I heard nothing. "Exactly!" he said. "There should be conversation, laughter, and a sense of fun here, not such silence. How can we be innovative with our products or engaging with our associates if it is so quiet? I need to help this organization change that." And he did!

Seek out ways to interject fun or play into the workplace. Some companies create informal social events and others simply make fun or play part of their daily lives. Look at ways companies raise money for United Way. There are ice cream socials, silly skits, and fun outings. I am reminded of a Minnesota company that planned an ice cream social for all employees and, as a surprise, rented a dunk tank for the event. And it was the company's senior leaders who lined up for dunking! The event raised a tidy sum for charity and the employees had great fun!

Being willing to appear out-of-character at an employee event, in a silly skit, or in a department video often comes with the territory of being a leader. Of course you can turn down such opportunities, but why would you if they're for a good cause and in good taste? I know a leader whose reputation as being approachable went up several notches when he performed in a company lip-synch contest!

Another organization we know took the "serious" work of their new success factor model and turned it into a Jeopardy game. Communicating a new initiative can happen in creative, engaging ways — just turn people loose on it, and you'll be amazed at the results.

As George Burns would attest, "Do what you love and you'll never work a day in your life." What type of workplace pulls you in? I'd bet it's one where you and others share a sense of fun, camaraderie, and common purpose in the midst of accomplishing great things. As the leader, you can make that happen!

Notes

Pay Attention to Your Attention

Are you good at multitasking? Many leaders are, and the fact is, they have lots of priorities and decisions to juggle, as well as office phones, cell phones, desktop computers, laptops, and/or iPads with all kinds of messages jangling for attention.

Yet with so many clamoring stimuli, do you consider your degree of attention toward others, whether in large-group or one-on-one settings? Those you meet with notice if you're giving more attention to the text message that just vibrated your phone rather than the person in front of you, and you are sending a message about what is most important to you.

Instead, consider this ground rule: whatever you are doing in the moment, be fully present for it. By giving others the power of your attention, you send a clear signal: "You matter to me, and this topic is important to me."

Ideas for Action

As a leader, what you say or do matters immensely to those around you — especially to those who report to you. Just as you expect the full attention of your direct reports during one-on-ones or team meetings, so, too, do they seek and deserve your undivided attention when presenting information or soliciting your opinion. Be sure you are not shortchanging them by being more responsive to a text message than to them.

Many leaders underestimate how much others pay attention to everything they say and do. You've probably had the experience of someone saying to you, "Well, you said that..." and being shocked to know that your seemingly offhand comment somehow became gospel. It's a hard lesson. A newly promoted senior leader said to me, "You mean I have to watch what I say now; I can't be myself?" Yes, you can "be yourself," but that doesn't mean you can say everything that occurs to you. Your words matter a lot; others may repeat them or act on them.

Your comments, actions, and body language convey powerful cues to others, who look for congruence. For instance, consider the CEO who proudly espoused an "open-door policy" and a desire to hear from others, but then communicated the exact opposite by having his office door physically moved so that his assistant would be anyone's first touch point. That was a message! Or the leader who spent much of her division meeting regularly checking her iPad in front of her team and answering e-mails, sending a tacit signal that distractions mattered more than her team.

Eye contact is powerful. We generally don't think about eye contact as being a leadership skill, but I think it is. You can either get someone to keep talking or be quiet through eye contact or lack thereof. How long do you wish to keep talking when the person opposite you is scrolling through their e-mails? Conversely, how valued do you feel when the person opposite you looks you in the eye and acknowledges what you say?

Upon his passing, the late Minnesota Twins slugger Harmon Killebrew was eulogized by fans and players alike, not just for his prodigious home runs, but even more for the attention he bestowed on those around him. "He was a consummate professional who treated everyone — from the brashest of rookies to the groundskeepers to the ushers in the stadium — with the utmost respect. I would not be the person I am today if weren't for Harmon Killebrew," said fellow Hall of Fame player Rod Carew.

I know some senior leaders who have banned open laptops, cell phones, and iPads from their meetings. Their mantra is, "if you need to step out to make an important call, do it — but don't destroy the importance of this meeting by being only half here." That's a clear message about showing up and paying attention.

The word communication comes from the Latin word *communicare*, meaning "to share." By sharing your attention with others, not only do you enhance the exchange of information, you set a positive example for others to follow. You have a chance, minute-to-minute, to show who and what is important to you. What's your choice?

Notes

Notes

Are You as Authentic as a 5th Grader?

This last year, I spent a day with two classrooms of 5th graders in Montana. Before walking into the middle school, I wondered what these eleven-year-olds would be like. The game show, *Are You Smarter Than a 5th Grader?* came to mind.

But my experience with these kids was not a lesson about how smart they were. I was struck by the fact that none were hesitant to be themselves. If they were touched by something they said it. Without filters or pretense, they were true to what they were experiencing. It was so delightful. Most 5th graders will tell you the unvarnished truth. It may not always be what you want to hear ("No, that tie doesn't look good."), but at least you'll know it's authentic!

With almost daily news stories about duplicitous leaders, authentic leaders stand above the crowd. They speak the truth, even when it may be difficult. They don't operate on pretense; what you see is what you get. When asked what they most admired in their best bosses, people will often say, "I always knew where I stood." That is authenticity in action.

Ideas for Action

Authenticity is sometimes wrongly perceived in business as a "soft" skill. However, authenticity can be even more important than financial acumen, considering its vital role in creating effective relationships with customers, shareholders, and employees. Why, then, do many leaders struggle with being themselves?

The most delightful part of my 5th-grade experience was how open these kids were — they had not yet learned all of the social rules or "politically correct" answers, which was okay. As adults, we somehow let rules dictate what we should say or do, but rules and fears can stifle openness. Fear of losing someone's approval means we may hide what we really think or feel.

Former Medtronic CEO Bill George believes business leaders purposely tamp down their authenticity because of cultural norms. "Many leaders — men in particular — fear having their weaknesses and vulnerabilities exposed," George writes in the *Leader to Leader Journal*. "So they create distance from employees and a sense of aloofness. Instead of being authentic, they are creating a persona for themselves."

You can't be authentic when you hide behind a persona. Your colleagues want to know about your reactions, thoughts, and feelings. I recall working with a marketing leader who others said lacked sincerity. She was devastated by that feedback, but eventually learned it came down to how she constantly sought input about what others were thinking without ever revealing what she thought or felt. Her co-workers were always left wondering: What does she think and stand for?

The common phrase "walk the talk" is also about authenticity. People pay attention to whether or not you live the values you espouse. If you talk about how important leadership development is for your team, do you personally reveal what you are doing to develop yourself? Do you spend time actively coaching those who report to you? You can apply that kind of questioning to all of the values you hold dear. Does your behavior or do your choices reflect them?

Even better, write down what you value as a leader. What is important to you? What kind of organization are you trying to create? What do you stand for? What kind of leader are you trying to be? Now for the hard part — ask those around you what you do that lines up with those values and whether you are doing anything that counters them. It is a great way to learn how others perceive your authenticity.

It's been said that authenticity is its own reward — a sentiment Shakespeare expressed in *Hamlet* 400+ years ago when he wrote, "To thine own self be true." In your heart, you know what you value and believe. Let the rest of us know too! That's authentic.

Notes

Notes

19

Skip Stones, Not Vacation

Many countries have a culture that expects and encourages vacations more than we do in the United States. If you have ever tried to connect with someone in Europe during August, you will find strong proof that Europeans believe in taking a break!

I am not advocating that we declare August "vacation month," but I am distressed when I see data that says Americans have on average three unused vacation days a year. The word *vacation* comes from the Latin word meaning "freedom." Since I love the work I do, I am not looking for freedom from it, but I would like the freedom for something: the freedom to relax, to spend time with friends and family, to explore new interests, or to have an adventure.

Vacations keep us physically and mentally healthier, providing new energy and creativity when we return to work. Leaders who really use their vacations send three clear messages to their colleagues: 1) "The world does not depend on me alone," 2) "Vacations are important for you too," and 3) "You can do things well without me."

Ideas for Action

Keep in mind the workplace adage: "What gets scheduled, gets done." Schedule and book your vacation time, and then keep it! Vaguely thinking you'll take a little time off doesn't work — there is always something that will seem more important. Plus, anticipating your upcoming break is part of the fun!

Don't just cross out the time on your calendar; give others advance warning so they can protect your schedule, too. Surprising your team in the middle of an important project doesn't allow them to do their best work, nor does it give them a chance to figure out how they will move things forward in your absence.

When you do finally get away, pull the plug completely! Constantly checking e-mails or staying connected to every decision is not really taking the break your body, spirit, and mind need. It defeats the whole purpose of getting away. As the *Wall Street Journal* recently reported, hotels offering "unplugged" or "digital detox" vacation packages are growing in popularity. Just imagine, at check-in you're asked to give up your digital devices and cell phones!

Develop a mindset that vacations are a necessary part of your leadership effectiveness. They are necessary to recharge your batteries, to see the world from a different perspective (even when you choose a "stay-cation"), and to return to work renewed and even more creative. Research shows that people who take vacations have a more positive mindset and outlook on life. Don't you owe that to yourself, your friends, and your family?

Notes

20

Practice Makes Perfect

A re great leaders born or made? While we know that some aspects of personality, drive, and intellectual ability are hardwired and a prerequisite to great leadership, in reality no one becomes a great leader without experience and practice. Just as athletic or artistic talent comes alive with practice, so, too, does leadership.

I have seen many executives advance their careers by making significant changes in their leadership approaches. Conversely, I've watched other executives grow stagnant by relying solely on what's worked in the past. But given the increasing complexity of our business world, every leader needs to embrace ongoing development and practice.

Ideas for Action

Leadership practice begins with intentionality and a commitment to improve on a regular basis. I recall hearing from Steve Uzzell, a former National Geographic photographer, on how capturing the ultimate nature image requires preparation, research, and opportunity. He quoted Louis Pasteur: "Chance favors the prepared mind." Like many things in life, unless you prepare, you won't know what to do when opportunity knocks. That same premise holds true for leaders. You need to practice and prepare for opportunities that come your way.

As reported in the *European Journal of Social Psychology*, researchers at University College London found that it took, on average, 66 days of daily practice before a desired behavior became automatic. While they found that skipping single days wasn't detrimental in the long run, early repetitions delivered the greatest boost in automaticity, before it eventually leveled off and became a habit.

To improve your odds of enhancing your leadership abilities through practice, create a personalized development plan. Divide it into sections: individual goals (self-improvement), team goals (relationship improvement), and organizational goals (organizational impact). Then, determine what you'll practice to achieve your goals. For instance: "I will be more open to new ideas and ask for more details before making a decision," or "I will contribute a new idea at each division meeting." You get the idea.

Solicit ideas for practice from your manager, peers, and direct reports. They will have ideas you may not have thought of and simply asking engages them in your ongoing development. As you progress, routinely ask the same people for feedback to ensure you're on the right track in what you are practicing. The surest way to re-peat bad habits is to assume you don't need any help learning new habits.

Look for other places to practice outside of your paid work. Sometimes it can be easier to try a new approach in a low-risk environment, such as in a community volunteer group or with a nonprofit board. Non-employer leadership op-portunities like these give you a chance to try out new behaviors and observe others' styles!

By regularly practicing desired leadership behaviors, you'll be prepared for opportunities and "chance" will be on your side!

Notes

21

Protect the "Vital Few"

W hether we are aware of it or not, leaders live in a constant battle between the important and the unimportant or between the immediate, close-at-hand, easily done task and the long-term, strategic effort. Leaders especially need to be mindful of "time eaters," because of how they drain resources, especially those of your team members.

The challenge lies in how you use your own time and, more importantly, how you help your team members make great choices about how they use their time and effort. The tyranny of the unimportant is a sneaky killer!

Ideas for Action

Try this exercise. Within the context of your organization's goals, list the top two to four things critical to the success of your organization and your team. Now, study your calendar. How does your use of time match with what is really important? Sit down with your team members, one by one and inquire similarly: How does their time usage map against what's most important? Your job is to help your team members use their time well.

When he coached the Los Angeles Lakers to four NBA championships, Pat Riley attempted to shield his teams from distractions he called "peripheral opponents" — the media, the hangers-on, and even the team's front office, at times. Instead, he wanted his players to focus solely on their task-at-hand: winning NBA championships. What do you need to shield your team members from? What are you doing to help them stay focused?

Make a list of all the peripheral opponents you can think of and ask your team to do the same. Figure out how you can collaboratively counter these.

Two years ago, one of our clients — a relatively young manufacturer of medical products — was just beginning to adopt a number of new processes and systems. There were multiple ideas and projects competing for attention. In fact, there was so much that nothing was really getting done. In response, the company's senior team began to distinguish between the "vital few" ideas and projects and the "great many." The company began doggedly and persistently focusing only on the "vital few." Within a year, the company began to progress, including increased employee satisfaction.

Expanding on this, be clear with your own team about the difference between "vital few" and "over-the-top" effort tasks. When you delegate a new task, encourage your team to ask you where the task fits in your list of priorities and what should go off the list if they take it on. Over-the-top effort tasks are those where you want someone to give 120%. There are other tasks where 80% really is good enough. Let them know the difference.

The ability to discern between what's really needed and what's merely nice was what author William Faulkner was getting at when he said, in reference to editing your own writing, that you must be willing to "kill all your darlings." While I don't normally use such extreme expressions, I believe you have to be willing to get rid of all your peripheral opponents to protect the vital few.

Notes

Embrace the Good Side
of Politics

In society and in business, the term "politics" carries negative connotations. And the expression, "play politics," implies someone who uses manipulation or deceit to get what he or she wants.

Yet, when I listen between the lines to why a leader has derailed, I sometimes hear comments like, "He was unable to navigate through the organization's politics." Or on the positive side, "We need someone who can handle the politics here," or "We need an individual who has good organizational savvy." Our French client calls it "organizational savoir-faire."

What is this elusive skill? In short, I think it is the ability to influence without authority and to read where the sources of power and influence lie. Great leaders work collaboratively with others to build coalitions, navigate special interests, create compromises, and negotiate conflicts.

Ignoring power and how it works is a recipe for disappointment.

Ideas for Action

Today's workplaces rely less on hierarchy and more on individual ability to influence and win commitment from others. Additionally, managers and professionals are often given greater responsibility without all the "authority" to get it done. Many of you work in organizations that are heavily matrixed. Who has power is not simply defined by "boxes" drawn on a page. These organizational structures require skills in negotiating with multiple stakeholders and learning how to influence without authority. In fact, our clients tell us this is one of the core skills they look for in new hires.

Whether you work in a matrixed organization or not, begin by analyzing your key stakeholders — those who have power and influence over your projects. Who is affected by your work, has authority over it, or has an interest in its outcome? This list could include your boss, your peers, your team, other co-workers, and even customers. Next, determine the power (ability to allocate resources) and interest of each of these individuals or groups. Then consider for each group or individual how well you know them, and how much trust you have built with each. Having solid relationships with individuals who influence your projects is part of navigating in a matrix.

Once you've analyzed your stakeholders, map their influence: create a visual model that shows those who influence and make decisions about your work. Realize that some of the "real influencers" may not be in your functional area. Stakeholders can influence in many ways, based on their expertise ("I know it"), their personality ("I have charisma"), their title ("I'm the CEO"), or their reward-giving ability ("I'm your boss").

Armed with such information, you'll be better prepared to influence or advocate for what you need. In some cases, you will need to find ways to align your interests with those of your key stakeholders. For others, you may need to build a relationship where none currently exists.

If you believe your job title defines the amount of power you have, you will have much less influence than you will need to get things done. Instead, by learning to influence and read the organization, you will gain greater commitment at all levels: direct reports, peers, and bosses. Now that's political success!

Notes

Shatter the Glass Wall

You've heard the term "the glass ceiling," a metaphor for an invisible barrier that exists between competent women and their documented lower percentage presence at the top of organizations. The "glass wall" is similar; it's the invisible barrier between women in staff leadership roles and their lower percentage numbers in more significant leadership roles. The glass wall takes away the very opportunity to be promoted to the top!

In a 2011 forum on Women and Leadership, sponsored by the *Wall Street Journal*, new research from McKinsey & Co. shows that "Qualified women actually enter the work force in sufficient numbers, but they begin to plateau or drop off when they are eligible for their very first management positions. And it only gets worse after that."

One of the ways we can counter this distressing trend is to help women broaden their experience and raise their hands for new opportunities.

Ideas for Action

If you're a leader and a woman, or if you manage women who lead, you can help address this talent shortfall by proactively working to ensure that women in your workplace receive ample development opportunities. This is not just about being ready to move up within one area; it is equally about breadth of experience. One of my clients told me a story about her manager asking her to consider a move from her HR role to a different role in the company, in order to gain broader experience. Her first response was, "Am I not performing well in this job?"

Helping women gain the breadth of experience that can set them apart for promotion is increasingly smart business, and indicative of a well-run company. As recent research studies indicate, when women are in an organization's senior leadership team, the company is likely to be more profitable, have a higher share price, and have more innovative research and development capabilities. The June 2011 issue of *Harvard Business Review* summarized research indicating a team's collective intelligence rises when more women are included. The same holds true for boards of directors.

My colleague Nancy Weidenfeller recently researched what it takes for women to achieve senior leadership roles. Her work was based on interviews she conducted with twelve disparate and highly successful female enterprise leaders. According to Nancy, the five most vital recommendations for women seeking to shatter the glass wall are:

1. **Seek out and gain profit/loss experience**
   - This was the single most important leadership development recommendation. Women should proactively pursue visible and impactful profit/loss responsibility.

2. **Consistently expect and exceed high performance**
   - Perform exceptionally in your current role to be in position to assume additional roles and responsibilities.

3. **Develop your self-awareness and authenticity**
   - Focus on aligning your inner values and outward behaviors and track your personal strengths and development opportunities.

4. **Build cooperative relationships**
   - Establish and leverage a "connect-and-collaborate" leadership style with peers, direct reports, and your supervisors.

5. **Become resilient and adaptable**
   - Learn how to become the "keeper of your own boundaries," set priorities, model a balanced life, and find supportive partners.

These five tips are actually applicable for all leaders, regardless of gender. However, by specifically practicing these, women in particular will more likely position themselves to advance their careers. Go for it!

Notes

Notes

24

One Size Does Not Fit All

L eadership is leadership is leadership. Or is it? Just because Steve Jobs was a high-impact leader for Apple does not mean he would have been a fabulous leader for Google. Just because a female colleague has demonstrated the ability to lead an operation through a significant change process does not mean she will be the right leader for seizing market share.

In business, context matters, whether you're selecting leaders or deciding how you want to lead in a particular circumstance or approach a specific individual. For example, I hope your approach with, say, the Italian sales team is different than the approach you would use with your Chinese suppliers. Try thinking about context and you'll be able to apply the right touch.

Ideas for Action

First, strive to understand the context and nuances of your organization by thinking carefully about the personality and goals of different parts of the organization. This includes paying attention to cultural and language differences and learning about what is accepted or respected. Even different parts of the same organization in the same geographic region can have different cultures. That is especially true in a conglomerate.

Second, get to know your colleagues as people and what matters to them. Observe their styles and think about how you might best adapt to them or work with them. In some respects, this is the heart of the concept of emotional intelligence (EQ). If I know myself well and understand others, I will be much more able to increase engagement and participation. Conversely, research shows that a primary reason leaders derail is a lack of interpersonal effectiveness.

Leaders adept at managing multiple types of employees are adroit listeners and effective communicators. They listen more than they speak, and skillfully expand the dialogue by asking great questions. When it's time to talk, these leaders can adapt their communication (and interpersonal style) to a variety of audiences and situations, ensuring their ideas are clear and actionable.

Many individuals we have worked with have found it helpful to use the work of Paul Hersey and Ken Blanchard, co-founders of the situational theory model. Their work espouses that effective leadership is task-specific, and that leaders need to adapt their style to the readiness level and experience of the individual or group they're seeking to influence. It makes great sense and their works provide a framework for action.

In the end, the best leaders are not those who impose their "style" on others expecting them to adapt. Rather, the best are those who work hard to choose a style that fits the context, the situation, and the people. Every day you have a chance to choose; make the most of it!

Notes

25

Uncover the Motivator

When organizations choose MDA to assess job candidates, one of the most common questions we hear is: "What makes him tick?" or "Why does she really want this job?" The question is perfect; you want to find the motivator. We can do that.

Yet, more often than not, the way to find out what jazzes someone or what they want to do long-term is to just ask! It is so easy to neglect this simple tool.

How often do you hear people "playing psychologist" by trying to assign a motive to a specific behavior? "He was quiet in this morning's meeting because he is bored," or "She hasn't raised her hand about advancement, so she is not ambitious." That may or may not be right. The point is, engage your team members in real conversations about their behavior and their goals; you will learn firsthand what is really important!

Ideas for Action

It is crucial for leaders to understand the motivators for their team members. The more care you take in aligning job roles and work environments to what motivates people, the more engaged they will be. And the more you find out what kind of work individuals find meaningful, the more you can deploy them in a way that brings satisfaction.

Rather than making assumptions about the type of work that people really enjoy, have one-on-one conversations with them on this topic. Find out what they are interested in doing; what jazzes them and what brings meaning to their work. It may take more than one conversation, but eventually you will create stronger connections with and for them.

Motivation is such a strong indicator of compatibility to specific jobs and environments that, during our assessment process, we use the MVPI (Motives, Values, and Preferences Inventory) developed by Hogan Assessments. It's a 200-question assessment that identifies an individual's core values — that is, what this person wants, as opposed to what they might do in certain situations. As Sharon Sackett, my colleague who runs our Talent Assessment practice, has said, "The more you can match what is important to an individual with what the job can provide, the more satisfied he or she will be."

What about money as a motivator? Of course money is part of whether someone is satisfied with their work, but it is a profound error to assume that it is always a motivator. Money can also be a dissatisfier — if I am not paid well enough I will be unhappy. However, money is not generally something by itself that makes an employee want to go above and beyond. Multiple studies, for example, have shown that many younger employees (Gen X and Gen Y) place compensation below such motivators as the chance to do meaningful work and having a balanced lifestyle.

While a tool such as the MVPI is powerful, if you'd simply like a current idea of what's important to someone, ask regularly. Even aspirations or career goals are not forever. Circumstances often change. For example: "Last year I did not want any more responsibility, but this year I can take on more and I am ready for a change."

Don't make one of the most common succession planning errors by assuming that your highest performer is "naturally" interested in moving up. Find out that individual's aspirations. You want to be sure that an eventual successor really aspires to moving up.

Think of how many workplace issues could be resolved simply by asking. Don't sit as a silent observer on the sideline. Ask away!

Notes

Built to Change

Built to Change — this is actually the title of a book by Chris Worley and Edward Lawler III of the Center for Effective Organizations at the University of Southern California. This phrase speaks volumes to all of us in leadership roles. Leaders need to be ready for change and able to lead it. Readiness means embracing change as a way of life and leading others confidently through it. Not just once, but on an ongoing basis!

Consider this: adaptability consistently shows up as one of the top traits organizations look for in their leaders. It means being hard-wired to see the world as ever-changing, being resilient in the midst of ambiguity, and helping others navigate change.

Ideas for Action

Admittedly, some people seem naturally better at handling change than others. While it is useful to consider how others react to change, at this juncture, focus on yourself first. Evaluate your typical reactions to change. Do you question it, avoid it, or explore it? If you tend to become stressed out during periods of change, find other ways to channel your energy. Acclaimed author and poet Maya Angelou once wrote: "If you don't like something, change it. If you can't change it, change your attitude. Don't complain."

Consider how much you embrace change on a daily basis. I had a professor in grad school who told us he would get nervous if he had not felt anxious or unsettled in the past month! Why? Because to him, it meant he had let himself get into a comfortable, easy rut. Try new ways of doing things — take a different route to work, vary your routine, explore another part of the city, interact with people outside of your circle — and you can increase your adaptability.

Practice the art of contingency planning. In addition to creating Plan A, have a Plan B (and C and D)! By preparing for change or unpredictability — adopting an "if this, then that" mindset — you will better steel yourself and your team to handle life's invariable surprises. And you'll be ready to capitalize on them!

When you are the one introducing and leading change, you know intuitively that it is essential to engage all who will be affected by the change: peers, customers, team members, other departments or functions, and your management. With our clients, we find it helpful to use a four-step model for leading change: Plan, Engage, Act, Sustain™. If you can help your team move through the change process following these four "simple" steps, you will increase the likelihood of a great outcome.

Being independent and resilient is a great attribute, but don't deal with change alone. Seek advisers — friends, bosses, or peers — to serve as valuable sounding boards. They can help you to discern opposing opinions, find new opportunities, and sift through them to arrive at the best choice(s) for action. The *Wall Street Journal* reports on a study indicating that incorporating advice from others improves decision-making accuracy.

The world will continue to hand us new challenges — it is our job to anticipate them, look for them, and adapt to them. Our future depends on it.

Notes

Where's Your Edge?

Recent times make it clear we live in the midst of uncertainty. Such uncertainty may tempt us to "play it safe" or to "wait and see" what will happen. Yet hesitating stands in direct contrast to being bold, or acting on your strong drive for leadership results. Great leaders don't let external circumstances dampen their drive.

General Electric under Jack Welch even had a leadership competency, simply called "Edge." It meant always looking for ways to improve, win customers, survive, and thrive.

Did you know that the Chinese word for crisis — *weiji* — is made up of two Chinese characters: "danger" plus "opportunity"? A leader's job is to constantly find, make, and seize opportunities — even more so in a sometimes dangerous, uncertain world!

Ideas for Action

In the late 1920s, two companies — Post and Kellogg's — dominated the emerging market for pre-packaged, ready-to-eat cereal. Then, the Depression hit. Post did the apparent sensible thing: it cut expenses and reduced its advertising. But Kellogg's — in a move now taught in business schools nationwide — doubled its ad budget, pushed into radio advertising, and heavily marketed its new cereal, Rice Krispies. By 1933, Kellogg's profits had risen nearly 30 percent and the cereal maker permanently surged past Post for market dominance. What will history say when it looks back on the moves your organization is making now?

Here's an historical example about individual leadership with an "edge": During the Civil War, Abraham Lincoln replaced the popular but ineffectual Gen. George McClellan as leader of the Union Army with Gen. Ulysses S. Grant, who eventually overcame multiple battle losses to win the war. When questioned early on about his selection of Grant, Lincoln simply explained, "He fights."

Results-driven leaders like Grant not only demonstrate their own personal drive to accomplish their goals, but also instill a sense of passion in others to achieve them. Are you leading with a sense of urgency and an edge? If so, don't simply assume that others will see your great example and copy you! Urgency might sometimes be contagious, but it often needs a boost. Think carefully about how you help others keep their edge in times of uncertainty, and always look for the next opportunity.

Set aggressive goals and timelines for your team while making sure the goals also pass the "realistic" test. Solicit early feedback from team members on the potential barriers to success, as well as resources needed. Create contingency plans and intervene when necessary.

Convene your team and brainstorm about opportunities. What have you, individually or collectively, been hesitant to do? Keep tabs on your competitors; what moves do you see them making? Stay close to your customers; how can you help them weather any storms they are facing? Look for examples of how other organizations have created or seized opportunities. Ask, "How can we do that here?"

Recognize that taking advantage of opportunities requires hard work; opportunities won't just fall in your lap. I particularly like this quote about opportunity from the prolific inventor, Thomas Edison, "Opportunity is missed by most people because it comes dressed in overalls and looks like work."

Find your "edge" in the midst of uncertainty. The opportunity is there for the taking.

Notes

Give Integrity a Voice

Everyone wants leaders with integrity — it should be the minimum price of admission to leadership. Yet with the seemingly endless corporate and political scandals we have witnessed, it is clear that integrity is not a given. Even though many organizations tout integrity as a core value, some still say it is in short supply.

If integrity is a core value for you, then don't hide it. How can others learn about your standards or what is important ethically if you are silent on the matter? Find ways to define integrity, talk about it, and highlight actions that display it. If you put integrity front and center in your conversations, it will have a strong ripple effect. There will be no question: this is how we do business here.

Ideas for Action

Share and repeat stories that show how you or others in your company have dealt with ethical dilemmas. For example, during his tenure as CEO of agribusiness giant Cargill, Warren Staley spoke frequently with employees and outsiders about the company's expectations for ethical behavior, including the challenges of doing business in other parts of the world. He exhorted people to operate with the utmost integrity while showing zero tolerance for anyone who violated the company's code of conduct.

Cargill put acquisition candidates to the same test. In an interview with *Chief Executive* magazine, Staley recounted that if the target company's ethics did not align with those of Cargill, his company declined the opportunity. He and Cargill had no interest in acquiring a business that condoned unethical behavior or looked the other way when it occurred. "It is very hard to compete against unethical people," he said.

Business integrity is also seen in smaller, day-to-day actions. Here are just a few of them: being transparent, owning mistakes, keeping confidences, being honest with customers and employees, keeping information about individual clients or patients confidential, maintaining accurate records, and competing fairly. What does it mean in your business and your world? Gather and tell the stories.

Bring ethical quandaries out in the open too. When have you encountered a situation where it took you a while to figure out the right thing to do? For example, a need for confidentiality can be at direct odds with a desire to be honest or transparent. Or a valued customer may make a request that you believe is inappropriate. What have you done or how have you handled the situation? Talk about it.

It would be wonderful if you could walk into work tomorrow ready to tell a story about integrity in your organization. If you don't have your own story to tell, use an example (good or bad) from the news and raise it as a discussion topic with your team: "Could this type of event ever happen here?"

By giving integrity a voice through regular workplace discussions, you will likely gain untapped reserves of support from employees and those outside of your organization.

Notes

Shhh — Don't Just Hear, Listen!

O ne day, our three-year-old granddaughter was trying to tell my husband something. She put her hand on his head and turned it toward her. "I want to see your eyes when I talk," she said.

Isn't that what we all want? Who among us does not wish to be heard and truly understood?

We are often masters at hearing, but not masters at listening. Hearing is about grasping the content; listening is about completing the communication loop and letting the other person know you got the message. I am constantly amazed by the number of leaders we work with who are told (and know) that they need to become better listeners. It's a simple skill that makes a difference.

Ideas for Action

Generally speaking — and speaking and speaking! — I believe that Americans love their conversations. That's why Starbucks has 11,000+ U.S. stores, Monday Night Football has multiple talking heads, and late-night talk shows try to keep us entertained. What's less clear is the amount of listening actually going on.

We work hard to say something in just the right way so it will be understood, but listening needs at least equal time and practice. Consider these cultural adages about listening, such as this Native American proverb: "Listen or your tongue will keep you deaf." Or the New England admonition (which I learned from the great John B. Davis, former head of Macalester College and the Minneapolis Public Schools), "Don't speak unless you can improve upon the silence." No relation to me, Davis was a well-respected leader and a true master of listening. He even kept detailed notes of what he had heard in meetings.

One of the ways to ensure you are a great listener is by asking superb questions that give you something to listen to! Ask open-ended questions, not simple questions that require only a "yes" or "no" answer. Try to stay away from unending strings of "Why?" questions, such as "Why did you do that?" or "Why do you think that?" It doesn't take much for people to think you are more interested in interrogating than listening. Far better is "What led you to that action or that conclusion?" You will learn a lot more from questions that show you actually want to understand.

Another tactic is to not interrupt someone in the middle of a thought. Not only is it rude and irritating, but it ultimately shuts down the conversation. Similarly, if someone comes to you with a problem, don't deliver a solution before your team member has finished speaking. Allow the full issue to be described and then ask, "What are you thinking about doing?"

To really complete the feedback loop, paraphrase or summarize the other person's key points or ask for clarification if something is unclear to you. Paraphrasing is a powerful tool that does two things: first, it lets the other person correct you if your recap is off; and second, it leaves the other person with the thought, "She understands me!"

In some cultures outside of the United States, there is more emphasis on non-verbal communication. Not just your gestures and facial expressions, but what you convey behind the words. There is even a Buddhist expression that states, "There is a truth that words cannot reach." Ask a trusted advisor how well your words are matching your intentions.

Finally, remember the power of eye contact. Even if you say nothing, your attention shows you care about what is being said. By regularly practicing your listening skills, something else seemingly magical will occur: people won't just hear your ideas, they will actually listen to them!

Notes

Notes

The Rewards of Reflection

I started these pearls with the premise that all of us are on a leadership journey of growth and change. If I were to say to you, "Tell me about a time when you learned the most about leadership," you would likely relate an experience. It might be a "first" or a "best" or a "worst" — but you would have a story to tell.

Your stories and your experiences create your own pearls of leadership wisdom. Yet these pearls remain hidden until you think about them. "We do not learn from experience, we learn from reflecting on experience," said the late psychologist John Dewey. A few moments of reflection or meditation every day can give you the insights to grow and change.

Ideas for Action

Even if you're not the reflective type, you can quickly learn. I was recently on an executive coaching panel at a professional conference with David Peterson of Google. Peterson, who has written extensively about coaching, extolled the power of reflection and suggested four basic tasks of reflection: to look inward (what am I trying to accomplish?); look outward (what matters to others?); look back (what new things have I tried?); and look ahead (what will I do differently?). That's it.

When I ask someone to take time for reflection, I often hear excuses: "I don't have the time," or "I don't like to write." Yet not all reflections need to be written down, just practiced regularly. Here is Peterson's formula for building a reflection habit:

1) Daily, for one minute
2) Weekly, for five minutes
3) Monthly, for 10 minutes
4) Quarterly, for 15 minutes
5) And annually, for one hour.

Even if this is all you can spare, you can tap into the power that comes from creating a habit.

Consider this: most leadership development programs, seminars, or initiatives now build in intentional reflection time (and it's more than just a minute or two!). There's sound science behind the practice. Physiologically, according to brain researcher James D. Zull, deep learning arises naturally from the structure of the brain itself. He points out that reflection engages the brain to search for connections — literally — to achieve comprehension. "Even if we experience something, it is hard to make meaning of it unless it engages our emotions," Zull says.

Reflection is particularly important when trying a new skill or having a new experience. Afterward, whether you simply think about the experience or write it down, you begin practicing the type of introspection that's characteristic of some of the world's greatest thinkers — and its greatest leaders!

Above all, reflection gives credence to the most important voice in your daily affairs: your own. As the late Steve Jobs counseled graduates in his famous 2005 Stanford University commencement address, "Don't let the noise of others' opinions drown out your own inner voice."

Take some time today to reflect, to hear your inner voice, and to learn. Your ongoing growth as a leader depends on it!

Notes

Notes

Notes

Suggested Reading

Bossidy, Larry and Ram Charan. *Execution: The Discipline of Getting Things Done.* New York: Crown Business, 2002.

Seligman, Martin E.P. *Learned Optimism: How to Change Your Mind and Your Life.* New York: Pocket Books, 1998.

Hersey, Paul H., Kenneth H. Blanchard, and Dewey E. Johnson. *Management of Organizational Behavior: Leading Human Resources.* 9th ed. Upper Saddle River, New Jersey: Prentice Hall, 2007.

Bibliography

Bughin, Jaques and Michael Chui. "The Rise of the Networked Enterprise: Web 2.0 Finds Its Payday." McKinsey & Company, *McKinsey on Business Technology* Spring 2011, no. 22: 2-3, http://lp.google-mkto.com/rs/google/images/EnterpriseWeb2.0.McKinsey.pdf.

Lally, Phillippa, Cornelia H. M. van Jaarsveld, Henry W. W. Potts, Jane Wardle. "Modelling Habit Formation in the Real World." *European Journal of Social Psychology* 40, no. 6 (2010): 998-1009.

George, Bill. "The Journey to Authenticity." *Leader to Leader Journal* 31 (Winter 2004), http://www.pfdf.org/knowledgecenter/journal.aspx?ArticleID=75.

"Leading Sustainable Change." MDA Leadership Consulting. http://www.mdaleadership.com/what-we-do/organizational-performance/sustainable-change/.

"MVPI." Hogan Assessments. http://www.hoganassessments.com/motives-values-preferences-inventory.

Silverman, Rachel Emma. 2011. "Some Managers Just Won't Take Advice." The *Wall Street Journal* (September 19). http://online.wsj.com/article/SB10001424053111904103404576560800619224540.html.

Tergesen, Anne. 2011. "When Guests Check In, Their iPhones Check Out." The *Wall Street Journal* online (July 5). http://online.wsj.com/article/SB100014240 52702304584004576417942784252336.html.

"A Blueprint for Change." The *Wall Street Journal* online (April 11, 2011). http://online.wsj.com/article/SB100 014240527487044151045762509000113069980.html.

Thompson, Mark C. 2004. "The Quiet Giant Speaks." ChiefExecutive.net. http://chiefexecutive.net/the-quiet-giant-speaks.

Woolley, Anita and Thomas Malone. 2011. "Defend Your Research: What Makes a Team Smarter? More Women."

Harvard Business Review online (June). http://hbr. org/2011/06/defend-your-research-what-makes-a-team-smarter-more-women/ar/1

Worley, Christopher G. and Edward E. Lawler III. *Built to Change: How to Achieve Sustained Organizational Effectiveness.* San Francisco: Jossey-Bass, 2006.

Zull, James. *The Art of Changing the Brain: Enriching Teaching by Exploring the Biology of Learning.* Sterling, VA: Stylus Publishing, 2002.

About the Author

SANDRA DAVIS is CEO of MDA Leadership Consulting in Minneapolis, a leadership development, talent assessment, and organizational performance firm she co-founded in 1981. Davis specializes in senior executive talent evaluation, CEO selection, and succession planning, and is widely known as an executive coach and thought leader in the industry, counting numerous Fortune 500 firms among her clients.

She earned her B.S. from Iowa State University and her Ph.D. in counseling psychology with an emphasis in industrial/organizational psychology from the University of Minnesota. She is the author of the book, *Reinventing Yourself: Life Planning After 50*, and has contributed numerous chapters and articles in professional books and journals on topics related to assessment, leadership development, coaching, and succession. She has been elected a fellow of both the Society of Industrial and Organizational Psychology and the American Psychological Association. She was named a "Women Change Maker" by the *Business Journal*, and she serves on the boards of multiple non-profits related to her passions for music and serving the poor globally.

In her free time, she enjoys outdoor activities, exploring diverse cultures, playing classical piano, and improving her mastery of other languages, including Mandarin.